BASIC BUDDHIST MEDITATION

BRIAN TAYLOR

道

UNIVERSAL OCTOPUS

Also available:

What is Buddhism?
The Living Waters of Buddhism
Buddhism and Drugs
The Five Buddhist Precepts
Basic Buddhism for a World in Trouble
Dependent Origination
The Ten Fetters (Saŋyojana)
Buddhist Pali Chants (with English translations)
The Five Nivāraṇas
(Buddha's Teaching of the Five Hindrances)

Published by Universal Octopus 2017
www.universaloctopus.com

Copyright © Brian F Taylor 1995

ISBN 978-0-9956346-9-5

CONTENTS

THE PRACTICE

T he goal of Buddhist Meditation is Nibbāna. It is not possible to realise Nibbāna unless one keeps the Five Buddhist Precepts.

This is because the precepts are designed to stop you causing suffering. Obviously you cannot free yourself from suffering if you are still actively causing it for yourself and/or others.

The precepts are statements of commitment to refrain from killing, stealing, misuse of the senses*, lying and taking drinks and drugs that cause carelessness.

Yet keeping these precepts is the outer shell of morality. It means one is restraining oneself from doing one or other of these things.

But if one is restraining oneself, it indicates that there is something to be restrained.

When one investigates this, one can see that before every act of killing, stealing, misuse of the senses, lying and drinking or taking drugs, there is a *mental* impulse to do these things. So long as these mental impulses arise, one cannot be sure that they will never lead to action.

The next step is, therefore, to purify the mind so that negative or unwholesome states will never arise in us again.

---

* See APPENDIX **A.** page 29

When this is achieved, human beings will have reached the first stage of human completeness or human perfection.

Or, to put it another way, human beings will be back to normal.

Purification of the mind is achieved by Insight Meditation. In Buddhist texts this is called Vipassanā.

Insight Meditation is a form of mental development. It is a kind of meditation that involves looking <u>inside</u> ourselves.

Normally our attention is turned outwards towards the world we live in. In this way we gather a lot of information and knowledge about the world. But we often do not know very much about ourselves. Because of this we are unable to free ourselves from suffering and unhappiness.

The method is to note, with full awareness, everything as it arises, in the present moment, at the sense doors.

There are six doors of perception:

The eye for sights
The ear for sounds
The nose for smells
The tongue for tastes
The sense of touch for physical objects
The mind for thoughts and states of mind

It is through these six sense doors that we experience the world. Without them we would experience nothing.

The method is simple. But it is not easy. If one can do it, one is face to face with reality itself, the actual continuous flow of one's life. If one perseveres, one comes, by degrees, to understand how everything works; how one's attention is caught by a sense perception and the mind is drawn towards it. How this outward reaching leads to actions through thoughts, feelings, words and deeds that have consequences for oneself and others.

The method is similar to focusing one's attention, minutely, on the detail of the images that appear on the cinema screen. If one can restrain oneself from being drawn into the story of the film, one comes to see that all these pictures, which succeed each other so rapidly, are none of them real; the fire is not hot, the water is not wet, the heroine is not a real girl.

Becoming disenchanted with the illusion of it all, suddenly one sees the screen behind it. Clear and bright and free from distracting images.

Similarly, when one becomes disenchanted with the endless flow of phenomena at the sense doors, one has a sudden and direct experience of Nibbāna.

The aim of Insight Meditation is the realisation of Nibbāna. Nibbāna is eternal peace and happiness, free from any suffering or unsatisfactoriness. There is nothing higher or better than Nibbāna.

According to this method, when something presents itself to our eyes, we note, "seeing". When a sound catches our attention, we note, "hearing". When our nose responds to a stimulus, we note, "smelling". When a taste presents itself to the tongue, we note, "tasting". When we become aware of physical contact with any object, such as our clothes or the floor under our feet, we note, "touching". When we experience sensations of discomfort, we note them for what they are: "itching", "aching", "stiffness", "tired", "hot", "cold". When thoughts come to our minds we note, "thinking".

Obviously, these things are going on all the time. But with Insight Meditation, instead of ignoring them, we deliberately direct our <u>attention</u> towards them and try to be aware of them while they are actually occurring.

Importantly, we do not make distinctions as to what exactly it is that we see or hear and so on. If we allow ourselves to particularise, we will be drawn into the detail, into trains of thought, and we will lose sight of the general nature of what we experience.

As far as the initial practice goes, it doesn't matter what you are looking at, it all comes down to just "seeing".

Consider a guard at the school gate whose job it is to try to prevent the students from carrying weapons into the school. His job is to see weapons and confiscate them. He doesn't need to particularise; gun, antique sword, razor, scissors, cosh, dagger. The detail doesn't concern him. He is just looking for weapons which might endanger other students.

So it is with seeing as just seeing, hearing as hearing, smelling as smelling, tasting as tasting, touching as touching, thinking as thinking.

While practising, we try to avoid being drawn into the details and being distracted by the associative thinking which these provoke.

Perceiving things in this way brings about an increasing detachment from the world around us. A centering of ourselves, a new stability.

When we have to move our bodies, we note each movement in two parts. First the intention to move. Then the actual movement itself: "stretching", "bending", "chewing", "reaching", "grasping", etc.

For convenience, the numerous activities that make up our lives from moment to moment are considered to occur in one of four postures:

Sitting
Standing
Walking
Lying down

When we are practising Insight Meditation, we can adopt any of these four. Meditators who are practising seriously for an extended period of time, usually alternate between a fixed period of sitting meditation and a similar period of walking or standing. Meditating lying down is fine too but there is a tendency to fall asleep. (Sleep is also fine but it doesn't lead to mental development and awareness.)

It is very beneficial to practise last thing at night and first thing in the morning.

Practising like this, we see for ourselves that all activities have two aspects, one is mental, the other physical. In this way, we are introduced to a fundamental principle of Buddhism. This principle appears in the Dhammapada in the Yamakavaggo section:

"Mind comes first."

It is because mind comes first that liberation is possible. If our characters and our behaviour were solely conditioned by our physical structure and genetic make-up, there would be no escape for us.

We would just be machines. Motorcars can't bring about their own development and become supercars. They need human engineers.

People blame their shortcomings on the fact that "they were born that way"; "that's the way they were made"; "that's how they were brought up". This then becomes a self-fulfilling prophecy. They say they cannot change and therefore they don't try. So it seems to be true.

If one is a brunette one may not be able to make oneself a blond without the help of hydrogen peroxide. But if one takes the trouble to investigate why one is a bad man or lazy or angry or violent or untruthful or a smoker or oversexed or shy or timid or arrogant or cruel or many other things that one would rather not be, one will find that all these characteristics arise first in the mind as a series of thoughts. These thoughts in their turn condition speech and behaviour. Repeated continuously, they bring about physical conditions that mirror them.

It is perfectly possible to arrest the flow of these thoughts, to let them go without allowing them to turn into words and actions and, ultimately, to replace them with thoughts and therefore characteristics that one would rather have instead.

One's present character is constructed of the mental building blocks of past thoughts, which continually arise in the present. This is how karma works. One can't change the past but one can learn from it. By working in the present, one can construct the building blocks of one's future character. This is how one uses karma to get what one wants.

But first, theory apart, one needs to see for oneself from moment to moment how it all works. One has to see the workings of mind and body. It is a practical process of continuous investigation, which provides the most amazing insights into life and the process of becoming.

The possibilities of self-development are truly endless. Rightly used, they certainly do lead to Nibbāna, the highest happiness, the deathless state.

Of course, Rome wasn't built in a day. How long a journey takes depends on how far away you start from. There are accounts in the suttas of men who completed the journey in less than a day. For others it has taken weeks, months, years or even lifetimes. That is karma again.

But one has to begin somewhere and some time. The method is available. But it is oneself that has to put it into practice, now.

YES

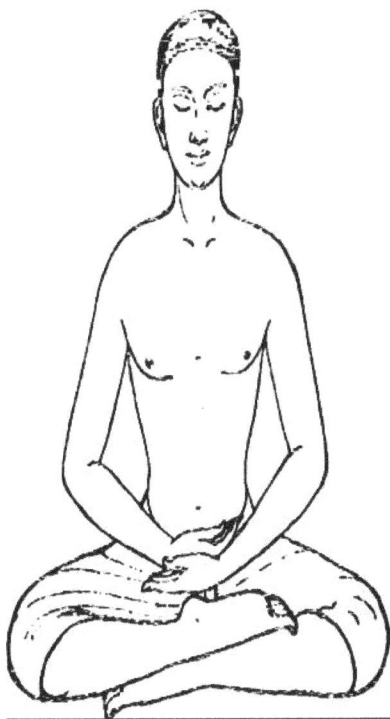

STOPPING THE MIND

If stopping were easy,
a thought beam
properly directed
would thread silently
through atom after atom
and bring the entire universe
to a standstill;
an empty mirror
reflected in itself.

If stopping were difficult,
the spider mind would jumble on,
piling thought on thought,
trapped in its own web;
the threads spreading out in all directions,
the atoms like so many jostling beads
dancing and tangling in ever clashing patterns,
keeping the entire universe
in eternally pulsating chaos;
a many-headed monster
glaring at its own reflections.

Not easy.
Not difficult.
A judicious response
to the Problem of Pain.

A letting go
of all phenomena.

Again.

THE METHOD IN DETAIL

Before one begins Insight Meditation, it is essential that one both understands and keeps the Five Precepts.

Keeping these precepts normalises one's relations with others by cutting off harmful actions directed towards them. It also gives one a basis for removing the impulses to harm others from one's mind. This is a great help in meditation.

If one is unable to come to terms with and keep these basic precepts it is not possible to come to a realisation of Nibbāna and so one's meditation practice will prove fruitless.

In this case, one would do better to concentrate on activities that help others, particularly the poor and needy. By doing this one acquires merit, which will be of use to one in the future. Helping others whose suffering is greater than our own also purifies the mind.

If we can sincerely accept the Five Precepts, we sit down straight and still, but relaxed. We pay attention to the movement of our abdomen while we are breathing in and out. We note the rising and swelling of the abdomen as we breathe in as "rising". We note the collapse and shrinking of the abdomen as we breathe out as "falling". We make no particular effort to affect the nature of the breathing as to its length or speed. We simply observe and note. "Rising". "Falling". The physical body is the object of this attention. The awareness itself is consciousness, which is a mental activity.

If the mind wanders and thoughts occur, we note them simply as "thinking". We do not follow them up or become distracted by the content of the thoughts. If feelings occur we note them as "feeling". If we experience discomfort we note it as "pain". A noise that distracts us is "hearing". Whatever catches the eye is just "seeing". If nothing catches the attention, we just continue to note the rising and falling of the abdomen.

The more we do this the more peaceful we become. Also we begin to notice where the breathing stops in the abdomen and where it begins again. Where the breathing starts and finishes is the very Centre of our being. It is the access point to where we and all living beings originated from. And it is the final end of all our sufferings.

Standing and lying down meditation are practised in a similar manner. The attention is directed towards the rising and falling of the abdomen and each movement is noted for what it is. "Rising", "Falling". Just as when we are sitting, anything that presents itself at any of the sense doors is noted for what it is and is not grasped after or followed up.

"Seeing". "Hearing". "Tasting". "Smelling". "Touching". "Feeling". "Pain". "Thinking". Et cetera.

If the position needs to be adjusted in any way, first the mental act of intention is noted, "Intending". Then the physical movement or sequence of movements. "Lifting". "Stretching". "Reaching". "Scratching". And so on.

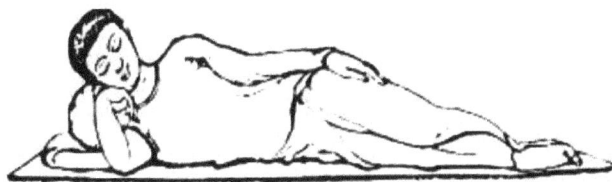

Walking is dealt with in a slightly different way. The walking is slow and controlled.

The attention is directed to the actual movement of the feet themselves. At first one notes "Left goes thus." "Right goes thus." "Left goes thus." "Right goes thus." When one is familiar with this, one can extend one's awareness so that it can take in the various movements of pressing, lifting, reaching and lowering which make up a complete step.

When one reaches the end of one's walkway one stops and practises standing meditation for a period. Then one notes the intention to turn, notes the various movements which are involved in turning the body round, stands for a while, notes the intention to walk and notes the walking back down the walkway as before.

This is an outline of a simple and basic method, which allows insight into the nature of things to develop in one's own mind. It is suitable for all, young and old.

If one perseveres, the mind becomes occupied more and more with the here and now and is weaned from its age-old habit of being triggered off into chains of associative thinking.

Everything slows down and is more easily observable as the mind becomes concentrated in the present.

One is intentionally withdrawing the attention away from the infinite detail of our lives back towards the Centre of our being. At this stage, one is withdrawing to the sense doors themselves and watching, carefully, how they operate and how the physical senses interrelate with the mind sense door.

One experiences a new kind of calm and peace, which is not related to, or dependent on, any sense gratification. Therefore, it is accompanied by detachment. Detachment makes it easier to observe the nuts and bolts of living impersonally; how the senses contact the sense objects and how the mind rushes out and grasps after them; how this leads to feelings, memories and associative thinking. One also has a glimpse of a state in which the mind is happy and peaceful and thinking can become a useful tool rather than a mechanistic master.

If one perseveres, one will experience a step-by-step deepening of awareness, which occurs in accordance with natural laws.

Some teachers have classified these steps, and even numbered them. A common classification is one into *Sixteen Steps to Enlightenment*. But these classifications have been made by the mind itself. One has to be careful to avoid getting caught in a mental net of expectation and then thinking the expectations have to be fulfilled in sequence.

It's quite possible to go from London to Rome via Paris and Athens but it's not obligatory. The main thing is to get to Rome. Details of a journey are just that; details, mental concepts, thinking. Meditators are not all alike. They have different individual characteristics. The speed at which they develop through the stages varies greatly and depends upon the amount of effort put forth by the meditator and the previous karma of the individual concerned.

No one, however, need lose heart. Nibbāna can be reached by anyone who keeps the Precepts and continues to note patiently each phenomenon as it presents itself at the sense doors.

It is difficult for anyone who is accustomed to thinking and distraction to see the profound significance of this Insight Meditation. But it is most important that it be persevered with.

THE THREE CHARACTERISTICS

While practising in this way, one comes to see that all the phenomena that present themselves at the sense doors have certain characteristics in common, irrespective of their details.

The Buddha has classified these characteristics as three:

All things are impermanent.
They are without any kind of self.
They are unsatisfactory.

IMPERMANENCE: Everything has a beginning and an end. Things come together, exist for a while and then disappear. They exist not as things in themselves but as collections of other things, which hold together and then fall apart. Nothing endures forever and unchanged.

In the physical world some things seem to last for a long time, such as planets and stars; others for a very short time, bacteria. But in the end, whatever comes together, falls apart again.

As far as the Practice goes, when we use our senses to evaluate the world around us, this is what we discover from personal experience. We see something for a while, then it vanishes. We hear something, then the sound stops. It is the same with the things we smell and touch. It is the same with the mind; thoughts come and go.

With the associative mind, one thought triggers off another, that thought yet another. We can think for hours and end up with a thought that seems to have no connection with where we started out. Often we can't remember where it did start.

Even our mental skills, our ability to organise thoughts into useful and meaningful patterns, fade away. We forget. We cannot concentrate. Our aged relatives cannot recognise us. They may not remember their own names.

In practising, we observe all these various phenomena which present themselves at the six sense doors and we come to the conclusion that everything that happens to us, moment to moment in present time, comes and goes, appears and disappears, is impermanent.

> Houses go from stone to dust.
> The builder is himself undone.
> The gate is broken, gone to rust.
> Nothing survives from sun to sun.
> What was there before the beginning
> lingers when stars now born are dead;
> in the absence of suns is ever shining,
> when nothing is thought and nothing said.

NOT SELF: Everything is without a permanent unchanging self.

There are bodies, which are made up of bits and pieces. These come together and fall apart again. The bits are then absorbed by other living beings. Everything in its turn becomes food for something else. If we want to think of our bodies as ourselves, we are free to do so. But we are talking about something that is unlikely to last more than eighty odd years, probably a good deal less.

CORPSE IN MY ROOM

An old machine
resting there
made of bits and pieces
whatever happened to be spare
of water, earth, fire and air.

An old machine,
connected to the mains,
switched on, is conscious of its pains.

Switched off, inert,
it does not know its ending;
lies in the dirt,
decays and rusts,
crumbles to dust,
uncomprehending.

As for our minds, our thoughts and opinions are a continuous changing flux over which we have little control and when we become old our memories fade and sometimes disappear altogether.

What of the harvest of that "inner eye"?
Even these mind-made facsimiles
will be lost in old age's imbecilities.

Body and mind are not ourselves. Nothing in the outside world is ourselves. Other people, nature, objects, houses, cars have their own existences independently of us. We cannot even think of them as our possessions except in a limited conventional sense. We have no ultimate control over them. They belonged to someone else once. They will again.

As far as the practice goes, prolonged observation of mind and body reveals that there is nothing in the nature of a permanent self to be found anywhere in either mind or body. There is just a continuous flux conditioned by karma.

At first this may seem disconcerting. All one's life one has been answering the question "How old are you?" by stating the age of one's body; or responding to comments like "He's intelligent" or "She looks a bit long in the tooth" as though they were made about a real enduring self.

But patient investigation reveals that there is no individual entity to be found anywhere in the flux of phenomena. The nearest one gets to it is the one who appears to be aware or conscious of everything that occurs.

However, when that is looked at more closely, it is seen that there is just awareness, just consciousness, which is indistinguishable from the awareness and consciousness found in beings in other forms of nature. Just as water in a glass is indistinguishable from water in a cup or a kettle. So when the feeling of being disconcerted passes (everything passes), one sees two things; one glimpses that if one could be without the whole flux of mental and physical becoming, one would arrive at an already existing state of peace; one also sees that, if there is no fixed unalterable self, we can develop and infinitely improve ourselves and achieve anything by using karma; *if this, then that.*

In the field of mental development, we plant the seeds which will produce the plants we want. We can *"rise on stepping stones of our dead selves to higher things."*

UNSATISFACTORINESS: Buddhism calls it Suffering.

> "Now this, monks, is the Noble Truth of Suffering: birth is suffering; ageing is suffering; death is suffering; sorrow, lamentation, pain, grief and despair are suffering; association with what we don't love is suffering; separation from what we love is suffering; not getting what one wants is suffering."

In short, life itself, made up of physical and mental experiences, is suffering.

Of course, we have always realised that life has its rough and its smooth side. We have taken the rough with the smooth, trying to extend what we like and limit what we don't like. But even the smooth turns out to be rough in the end for, when we get what we want, we experience that it doesn't last or we lose it or it is taken away from us. Or we die away from it. Or we find that *we* change and we no longer want it (all divorces were preceded by marriages).

Life starts with a birth and ends with a death. In between there is an unstable up and down, over which we do not have control. We do not even know that we will wake up tomorrow.

> Ever so long ago. Today.
> And ever after.
> Your tears will wash away
> your broken laughter.

As one goes on practising, one's own experience confirms the Buddha's teaching; *everything* reveals these three characteristics.

By patient observation, one comes to see that the endless flow of phenomena that presents itself at the sense doors is undesirable. This seeing that something is undesirable causes the desire for it to fade. One's understanding is getting closer to matching one's experience until they equate:

I see it as undesirable and I do not desire it.

One turns away from what one no longer desires. One realises that the increasing peace and calm which has been growing inside one as a result of improved concentration and the weakening of the restless, distracted mind, is the gate to Nibbāna itself.

Providing one continues this practice of noting and understanding, irrespective of what phenomena, pleasant or otherwise, may arise, one's progress towards permanent attainment of the Supreme Goal, Nibbāna, is assured. One should never be satisfied with anything less, however enticing it may be, that one meets on the path. Whatever it is, it will always, upon investigation, reveal the three characteristics.

THE STAGES OF PROGRESS

The practice of Insight Meditation takes one further and further back into one's self towards the Centre, one's ultimate beginning. It is like riding backwards on an elephant. One leaves the point one has reached now by moving out and starts going backwards and inwards to the beginning of it all. Voluntarily.

One experiences some truly remarkable things first hand, which cause one continually to adjust one's viewpoint. This adjusting and expanding viewpoint gets closer and closer to mirroring how things actually are rather than how one wants them to be. Or how others have told us that they are.

It is as though one enters a cave leading to the centre of a great mountain from which one emerged a long time ago. One's aim is to reach the centre but one passes so many interesting things, some of which one recognises, and they catch one's attention.

How quickly one reaches the Centre, depends on the speed at which one moves. The slower one moves the more things one sees to be distracted by. How fast one goes depends on one's concentration, one's determination and the degree of understanding one already has when starting out. In other words on one's previous karma.

So what is one trying to achieve? One is trying to put an end to all suffering. Just that. One continually examines the way in which the mind reaches out towards sense objects because it finds them desirable and how it continually experiences dissatisfaction, either immediately or later. This is the red-hot poker lesson.

One reaches out for the red-hot poker, grasps it and gets burned. Over and over again. Until the repeated pain gives rise to a meaningful Why? How? One investigates, thoroughly and persistently, until at last one sees the whole process. If this, then *that*. If not this, *not that.*

When this is seen, desire spontaneously evaporates. If later one forgets (flesh heals, one forgets), one resumes the process of examination. Over and over and over again until one's understanding, which has been wavering, finally equates to one's experience, which is always the same, and one is free.

I see it as undesirable and I do not desire it!

Buddhism teaches that our bondage is due to Ignorance and Compulsive Desire.

Ignorance is not knowing, not seeing, not understanding, from moment to moment, the fact of suffering and the cause of suffering.

Compulsive Desire translates a Pali word that is usually translated as Craving but really means Thirst. If one thinks of the compulsive thirst of the alcoholic, one is not far off the meaning.

The root of craving and thirst is Desire. One desires things that ultimately cause suffering because one finds them desirable. One wants to win so one ends up losing. One wants to drink so one gets a hangover. One smokes dope to get high so one gets addicted. One wants the bait so one gets the hook. One wants to be born so one grows old, gets sick and dies. The moment suffering and understanding balance out, desire on that level evaporates and one is free.

The first stage is reached when one's desire for renewed physical existence wanes. One becomes convinced that the objects of the five senses are always ultimately unsatisfactory. They enslave a man without ever giving him the complete and permanent satisfaction that he seeks. To experience them one has to go through the process of birth. When one no longer wants them, one no longer wants to be born. One turns away from physical existence. One will not be born here again.

The second stage is reached when one has the same realisation about the desire for mental existence. Mental states, however refined and exalted, reveal, on investigation, the same three characteristics, though in a much more subtle form. They also act as entry points to higher planes of existence, of which there are many. These are more subtle but even more binding.

One can no longer say that they are worlds of suffering. They are too subtle, too refined, but they are still certainly unsatisfactory. On the highest plane, the unsatisfactoriness has been reduced to a barely perceptible boredom and an awareness that, even here, things, though they undoubtedly last a long time, do not last forever. They are impermanent like everything else. And when the accrued merit that gives one entry to them has been used up, one falls away to lower levels again.

The final stage is reached when the subtlest desire of all, that for individual existence, is identified as the ultimate bondage which binds us to the wheel of becoming. *If this, then that.*

If I want to be something, later on I will have to lose the something that I become. Everything that has a beginning has an end. For millennia, this urge to be a separate entity, to have a separate consciousness, to be in some way different and individual, has bound us to wandering on from birth to death to rebirth.

Whatever has a beginning has an end. When this is understood and the desire for "I Am" is relinquished there is just an unimaginable and indescribable permanent Peace, which has been here forever.

Permanent? But isn't every thing impermanent? Yes, but *this* state is in no way a *thing*. It has never had a beginning and therefore it has no end. It really has to be experienced for oneself. Thinking cannot reach it. And it is not Death.

The Buddha lived and taught for forty-five years after his Enlightenment. A man who has realised Nibbāna doesn't just drop down dead. His body continues the normal ageing process and is vulnerable, as all bodies are, to injury, illness and ultimately death (whatever is born dies). But all the sources of mental suffering have been cut off. There is nothing in which unwholesome states of mind can take root. The craving for future existence is extinct. Peace and happiness are present in the here and now.

When the body eventually dies, there will be no more becoming whatsoever.

HERE

Now
runs like a crack
through the universe.

Through it
beings escape.

Between each step
Between each movement
Between each breath
Between each heartbeat
Between each living cell
Between each thought
Between each impulse,
Light shines;
through the crack
that runs through
the universe NOW.

No-one who grasps after
even a speck of dust
(even his own shadow)
can squeeze through this crack.

THE QUIET MIND

The sun
shines
in a bucket of water

but doesn't
get
wet.

APPENDIX

A. *P.1* "...misuse of the senses ..."

This is the Third Precept:

I undertake to refrain from misuse of the senses.

KĀMESUMICCHĀCĀRĀ VERAMAṆĪ
SIKKHĀPADAṀ SAMĀDIYĀMI.

KĀMESUMICCHĀCĀRĀ literally and originally means: *misuse of the senses.* That is, <u>any</u> of the senses. Later, and especially recently, it has acquired the more limited meaning of *sexual misconduct*, which is variously interpreted by different cultures and in different places. Misleadingly, this has acquired the status of a standard English translation.

Originally, the function of all the five senses is to contact the outside world.

The function of the Mind sense is to interpret their perceptions and relate them to acquired or inborn knowledge in order to promote survival and avoid non-survival.

Then, Ego appears as a result of <u>false identification with mind and body</u>, this gives rise to the erroneous belief in the existence of a separate self.

The Buddha corrects this fundamental error in his teaching of anatta.

Everything is empty of a separate self.

The problems caused by the Ego are covered in the Ten Fetters, numbers 1. Sakkāya-ditthi and 8. Māna.

The Ego is all about liking and disliking, wanting and not wanting. The mind becomes polluted by this and, since "<u>mind comes first</u>", the polluted mind uses the five senses to seek out sense objects which entangle itself even further.

It is not only sexual lust which is meant. It is any sense contacting any sense object and setting up a chain reaction with the mind of interactive pollution.

In the *Kilesa-saṃyutta,* the Buddha specifically states that <u>any</u> association of "desire-passion" (*chanda-rāga*) with the body or mind is a "defilement of mind" (*cittasse'so upakkileso*).

Of course, this includes adultery and paedophilia, and, depending on views prevailing at a given time, perhaps even LGBT! But it is much more than that.

Think of those Roman gluttons who, having eaten as much as they could, took an emetic, vomited it all up and returned to the table for more! Think of the youngsters going everywhere with earphones full blast with discordant music. Think of Cleopatra and her vials of perfume. Think of drunkenness, drug addiction, body piercing, masochism... "news"papers, TV...

B. The Ten Fetters* *(Saŋyojana)*

1. Sakkāya-ditthi: "Own body views".

In the commentaries, which are all later than the Buddha's teachings, it is said that sakkāya corresponds to sat-kāya, "existing group" and not to Sanskrit sva-kāya, "own group" or "own body".

---

* *The Ten Fetters (Saŋyojana) ISBN 978-09571901-1-5*

However, it makes better sense to see it as equivalent to sva + kāya = "own" + "body", where "body" refers to both the physical body and the mental body.

In most English versions, sakkāya-ditthi is translated as "personality belief" but this is too imprecise and tends to suggest to western students that they don't exist, which they often don't find very helpful.

What is meant is that any *opinions* (views) about the mind and body complex make one think of it as some kind of self or possession. Since mind-body is the source of all suffering, one will never achieve liberation from it while one hangs on to opinions about it; such as it is oneself or can be possessed by oneself. With thoughts like these, one will never entirely let go of attachment to mind-body. What is required is investigation of how mind-body is constructed in terms of the five khandhas*. Full understanding of these is followed by letting go.

8. Māna: "Conceit".

This is generally translated as "conceit" or "pride". "Conceit" means "an exalted conception of self-worth". Māna can be both gross and subtle. It appears as asmimāna, the conceit of "I am": i.e. "I exist as a separate physical or mental entity". It is an underlying tendency (anusaya) to compare oneself with others in ways where one is identifying oneself with own mind or own body.

Comparison is in itself not a fetter. I can say, "I am bigger than he is or older or speak more French." But these may be simple conventional matters of fact, similar to "He has red hair, I have brown" or even

---

* See **C.** *The Five Khandhas page 33*

"His hair is redder than mine". It is when I identify with something which may or may not be a fact, but which I grasp after as in some way belonging to me personally, that the fetter arises.

It arises in three forms: I am better than him; I am equal to him; I am not as good as him. Each of these may be matters of fact. However, one needs to be aware of the mental state that accompanies them to see if there is any trace of self-exaltation or self-satisfaction. One often meets people who are insistent that they are not as good as someone (Jesus perhaps. Or Joe DiMaggio). This may well be true but, if they take undue satisfaction in their humility, it will, on examination, be found to be not humility at all but inverted pride.

It is clear that māna depends upon duality. But ultimately, everything is a unity. We are all part of the whole whether we realise this or not.

One can visualise the whole universe as an octopus and all living beings as the tentacles. One can see that, fundamentally, under the influence of māna, a tentacle is comparing itself to another tentacle. It is ignorant that the origin of all tentacles is the Centre. No tentacle can ever be entirely separate.

"There being really no duality, pluralism is untrue."

The *fetter* consists in being bound to (holding on to) a secondary level of being, the level of duality and plurality.

C. The Five Khandhas *(groups, aggregates):*

Rūpa (material forms or body)
Vedanā (sensations or feelings received from form)
Saññā (perceptions)
Saṅkhāra (mental formations)
Viññāṇa (consciousness)

The Buddha explains that, in the absence of a self as a separately existing entity, these five factors constitute and completely explain the whole of a human being's mental and physical existence.

They are, therefore, the basis for all our suffering.

Close examination of them in our life continuum provides a continuous demonstration that, like Peer Gynt's onion, when investigated, there is to be found in mind and body, no trace of a permanent, enduring individual soul or self.

The gate to Freedom from Suffering is wide open.

www.ingramcontent.com/pod-product-compliance
Lightning Source LLC
Chambersburg PA
CBHW020445030426
42337CB00014B/1400